Old Rubislaw, Hazelhead and Manr
Patricia Newman

Snow came to Hamilton Place and so did sheep in this photograph. At one time, it was common to see sheep, cattle and pigs being driven through the town to the slaughterhouse in Hutcheon Street or to the mart at Kittybrewster. Westburn and Victoria Parks closed their gates when animals were on the move to prevent them straying off the road onto their carefully tended lawns and flowers.

Acknowledgements

David Main and David Oswald, Aberdeen Library and Information Services
Sandy Whyte (sadly now deceased) and Hugh Black owners of Rubislaw Quarry
Ian Murray for help with identifying machinery at Rubislaw Quarry
Allan Condie for his knowledge of trams
Rosie, Ian, Jen, Bill and Dave for help and encouragement.

Patricia S. Newman.

The publishers regret that they cannot supply
copies of any pictures featured in this book.

Printed by
Berforts, 17 Burgess Road, Hastings, TN35 4NR

Children and adults enjoying a sunny day at the park. Hazlehead Café – formerly Hazlehead House – is in the background. Two couples are dancing on grass on the right, an impromptu waltz in the woods. After the Second World War there was a dance floor in the park. The ladies and the older men are wearing hats even when relaxing as was the fashion then. There are a number of cloche hats which were popular until the early 1930s so I would think that this photograph dates from the 1920s.

Introduction

The area covered by the photographs in this book is extensive. All of it is outwith the original boundaries of Aberdeen which have been extended and redrawn several times as the city expanded. In 1871 the boundary was redrawn to include North Broadford (the area north of Hutcheon Street), Fountainhall, Mannofield and Broomhill. Further extensions brought in Hazlehead and Ruthrieston.

Historically, much of the area was either owned by the city as part of the Common Good or Freedom Lands granted to the city by Robert The Bruce and subsequently extended (and sometimes contracted) by the city, or by various wealthy families including Menzies of Pitfodels to the south and southwest and the Skenes of Rubislaw to the west.

As part of Aberdeen's extension westwards, the estate of Rubislaw was bought by the City of Aberdeen Land Association (CALA) in 1877. Ironically, Rubislaw had been part of the Freedom Lands but was sold to the Skene family when the city needed money. Under CALA's ownership, the area was developed with new streets and feus for housing.

Of course, the area is noted for its granite quarry. Opened in 1740, Rubislaw Quarry was the second granite quarry in Aberdeen, the first being Loanhead at Mile End. Estimating the quantity and quality of stone that might be obtained from a quarry was extremely difficult and required considerable expenditure for an unknown return. In fact, such was the primitive knowledge of geology then that a speculative coal mine was sunk unsuccessfully. However, around six million tonnes of granite have been extracted from this quarry in its 200 year life. It has been estimated that 50% of the buildings in Aberdeen were constructed of Rubislaw granite and the stone has been exported all over the world to enhance buildings.

In the early years, Rubislaw was not just one quarry but several until John Gibb acquired the leases for all the workings in 1830. Gibb was born in Falkirk in 1776 and orphaned when young. He was apprenticed to John Rennie, a noted civil engineer. While he was employed by Rennie, he worked on the new harbour at Greenock and the Lancaster Canal. Subsequently, he worked for John Dalgleish Easton on the docks at Leith. In 1809, while working on the dock at Greenock, he impressed Thomas Telford and was employed by him to supervise work on the harbour at Aberdeen being given the title of Permanent Superintendent of the Harbour Works at a salary of £250 per annum. During the nine years he

worked in this capacity, he supervised the restoration of Smeaton's Pier, the extension of the North Pier and the creation of a south breakwater. His interest in quarrying arose from his need for quality stone in his harbour contracts. While working for Telford, he met the poet Robert Southey who described him as "that obliging, good-natured, useful and skilful man, Mr. Gibb." Among other projects, he worked on the Bridge of Don, Potarch Bridge, Peterhead Harbour, the Crinan Canal, Dean Bridge in Edinburgh and Wick Harbour.

Rubislaw Quarry closed in 1971, the last quarry to close in Aberdeen, and was purchased by two Aberdeen businessmen in 2010. It is planned to turn the historic site into a visitor attraction.

To the west of Rubislaw lies the 832 acre estate of Hazlehead. It was bought by the city in 1920 for the reputed sum of £40,000 from the estate of William Rose of the shipping firm Donaldson Rose to create a public park. It is within the Freedom boundary of the city and was feued out in 1553 following the issue of a licence granted in the name of Mary, Queen of Scots in 1551.

Further south lies Mannofield, also part of the Freedom lands and known as the Foul Moors until, in 1772, Robert Balmanno purchased and drained the area providing rich earth for the growing of fruit and vegetables. His strawberries were said to be the best in Scotland and were sold in Covent Garden in London. As a Quaker or Friend, he named his new home Friendville and the area became known as Balmanno's Field, later shortened to Mannofield. A village grew up on the road through the estate and was called Mannofield. It was a separate village until the Aberdeen Municipality Extension Act of 1871. In 1882, the city extended the gas supply to the area.

Around Mannofield, the Menzies family of Pitfodels held land for several centuries before the family died out and the land went out of their ownership. Their estate included Braeside, Ruthrieston and Kaimhill.

The photographs in this book illustrate a prosperous residential area with fine churches, granite terraces and substantial detached houses. Public transport has been provided first by trams and later by buses with easy access to the city. Previously outlying areas have been absorbed into the city, making use of granite to provide buildings that are unique to Aberdeen.

ABERDEEN YOUTH HOSTEL   411

The youth hostel is at 8 Queen's Road. Built by John Rust in 1895 as private housing, this was originally a double villa that was converted into a single dwelling around 1930. In 1928 the Grammar School purchased No. 8 Queen's Road, calling it the "Grammar School House". Here boys attending the Grammar School could be boarded during school terms. A short time later, Nos 8 $\frac{1}{2}$ and 6 Queen's Road were bought and a new wing added. Grammar School House closed in 1956 and the Grammar became a day school. In 1957 the house was opened by the Scottish Youth Hostels Association who called it the King George VI Memorial Hostel. The building continues to provide hostel accommodation.

In 1925 Albyn Place School moved to its present location in Queen's Road and became the Albyn School for Girls. The school has since expanded into adjacent villas and now occupies 17, 19 and 21 Queen's Road. The school gradually became co-educational from 2005 when the first boys joined Primary 5 until full integration in 2013. The original building – No. 19 – designed by Matthews & Mackenzie in 1882, is category B Listed and considered to be of regional importance. The school was known locally as Mackie's or later, Miss O's (Miss Oliver's) after the head teachers of the time.

FRONT ENTRANCE, CONVENT OF THE SACRED HEART, ABERDEEN

The Convent of the Sacred Heart at 3 Queen's Cross was founded in 1895. The society originated in France in 1800. While the impressive building we now know was under construction, lessons were held in the gardener's cottage in the grounds. In the first year, it was a primary school (St. Joseph's) and then a secondary school (Our Lady's) was added in 1896. From 1907 until 1932 there was also a teacher training school. Eventually, dormitories were added for boarders. Mother Anne Welsh, Mother Superior, was only 33 years of age when she founded the convent but died three years later from influenza. In 1971, the secondary school closed and St. Joseph's became a local authority primary school in 1973, the building being leased to Aberdeen City Council. There are now no Catholic secondary schools in Aberdeen but Catholic religious education in three non-denominational secondary schools with Catholic pupils continues to be made available by the sisters.

SOUTH FRONT FROM THE WEST, CONVENT OF THE SACRED HEART, ABERDEEN

This view of the convent shows the beautiful ashlar granite with which it is constructed. The building was probably designed by J Russell Mackenzie with later additions on the left of the photograph by J Devlin in 1911. The Devlin extension includes a modestly appointed chapel. The buildings comprising Nos. 1, 3 and 5 Queen's Road and 3 Queen's Cross are listed Category B along with the walls, gates and gate piers.

At the junction of Forest Road and Queen's Road stands this grand double villa, numbered 2 and 4 Queen's Gate. The property is Listed Category C – a building of local importance. No. 2 Queen's Gate, on the right, was formerly owned by Miss Harriet Warrack, founder of Albyn School. For a time this was where boarding pupils stayed. No. 4 Queen's Gate was an elementary and preparatory school for girls in 1884. It had originally been housed at 2 Argyll Place and moved to Queen's Gate around 1903 when the school extended its remit to provide education up to university level. At Queen's Gate, the principal was Miss Margaret Duncan Jarvis. Latterly the school was presided over by its principal teacher, Miss Lippe. It flourished for a time as a senior school in the early years of the 20th century, closing in June 1919 when Miss Lippe retired. It had been successful in preparing girls for university education at Oxford, Cambridge and Aberdeen.

412 Forest Road from Queen's Road, Aberdeen. "Adelphi Series"

Forest Road runs from Queen's Road at Queen's Gate, as seen above, to King's Gate, crossing over the North Burn of Rubislaw. The street was named after the Forest of Stocket. The house on the left of the photograph is 6 Queen's Gate. It is the end house of a terrace in Forest Road designed by Matthews & Mackenzie in 1877. The terrace is listed Category C. This house like many others nearby has been converted into offices. Many of the houses in Forest Road are listed as being of architectural merit.

This view of Queen's Road shows a tram destined for Castle Street with a board advertising Fred Hardie's photographic studio at 416 Union Street. The studio was advertised from the first decade of the 20th century until the 1920s although latterly it was run by Mr. Hardie's widow. On the left of this view are three near identical houses numbered 60 to 64, designed by John Rust around 1901 and Category B Listed. The traction pole on the left is a support for the tramway cables. This line is single track but passing loops would have allowed trams to pass one another.

QUEENS ROAD, ABERDEEN.

Queen's Road looking east with house No. 53 with the central conical turret on the far right. All these houses were built as private residences but most became impracticable due to their size and were converted into hotels and offices. On the right, 51 and 53 became the Queen's Hotel to be joined later by No. 49 and renamed. On the extreme left is No. 50, a marvellous confection of different styles. It was built by John Morgan as his own home. It is thought that he also built 49, 51 and 53 to a design by A Marshall MacKenzie. 53 was a speculative build by Morgan who advertised it for sale in 1896. A horse-drawn cab can be seen to the right of the photograph with the cabbie asking the passenger for his destination.

The property called Bay View House is out of sight at No 86 Queen's Road although this area is sometimes referred to as Bay View. The building on the extreme left of the photograph with the elaborate gate posts is 96 Queen's Road. Formerly the Earl's Court Hotel, it was originally a private house designed by Robert Gordon Wilson of Ellis and Wilson in 1898. This Grade B listed building has since been converted into flats. As the tramway traction poles can be seen in the distance, this photograph must have been taken after the tram lines to Bay View House were laid 1896 but before the extension to Hazlehead in 1924. The house second left is 94 Queen's Road, a private residence designed by George Coutts in 1899. He also designed Nos. 90 and 92. Still in private ownership, 94 has seven bedrooms and six public rooms.

THE RUSTIC BRIDGE, JOHNSTON HOUSE, WOODED DEN, KEPPLESTONE, ABERDEEN

4037

The Johnston Estate was once owned by George Birnie, a native of New Machar in Aberdeenshire. He emigrated to Charleston, South Carolina, where he was a merchant for some years. He then came home to Scotland and to the Johnston Estate where he died in 1871. The estate passed to his son, John B L Birnie, an advocate and author of legal texts in Edinburgh. Johnston House was then let to a succession of tenants including Alexander Johnston, Writer to the Signet. His wife Christina was the daughter of John Leith Ross of Arnage. Christina died of typhoid fever at Johnston in 1878. Her husband, Alexander, died in 1880 at Foveran House. Later it was the home of J Forbes Lumsden of the Balmedie Lumsdens. In 1936 the estate was broken up and Johnston House disappears from the records. However, the gardens attached to the house were given to the City of Aberdeen and have been a source of pride to Aberdonians. In 2002 the park won the Britain in Bloom Public Park Award. The park lies to the south of Queen's Road near the Gordon Highlanders Museum. At just over two acres, it is small for a public park but its colourful shrubs make it a popular spot for wedding photographs. The Westburn of Rubislaw runs through it and on old maps there is a mineral well or chalybeate marked.

ENTRANCE LODGE, HAZELHEAD, ABERDEEN. 202543

Hazlehead Park is in the area of the Freedom Lands granted to the people of Aberdeen in 1319. In 1553, along with other land, it was feued out under licence granted by Mary, Queen of Scots to burgesses, inhabitants and traders in Aberdeen. This meant that it could be rented out to provide an income for the Common Good Fund. However, on several occasions, Aberdeen was in desperate need of funds and the land passed out of the ownership of the City. In 1920, following the death of Donaldson Rose, a wealthy merchant and ship owner who owned Hazlehead, the city council purchased the Home Farm, mansion house and estate from his trustees for £40,000. It was opened to the public in April 1821 with a bus service to take travellers from the Rubislaw tramway terminus to the park. Later, the tramway was extended to Hazlehead. The No. 4 tram took generations of Aberdonians to the park and the playing fields. The entrance lodge seen in the photograph was designed by John Smith around 1826 in a mock tudor style. It is a Grade B listed building. The park covers an area of 180 hectares and as such is Aberdeen's largest public park. It has wonderful mature trees and shrubs, including some magnificent rhododendrons and azaleas. There are football pitches and a golf course and there is a maze for folk to get lost in. On a sadder note, there is a North Sea Memorial Garden which commemorates all those who have lost their lives there. The centre piece is the Piper Alpha Memorial to 167 men who died on that rig.

THE CAFE, HAZLEHEAD, ABERDEEN

Hazlehead House was built in the 1700s as the mansion house for the Hazlehead Estate. For many years, it was the home of the Rose family who were eminent shipbuilders and ship owners in Aberdeen under the name of Donaldson Rose and Company. When the city council bought the estate to create a public park, it was decided to advertise the house to let as refreshment rooms. In 1921 it was leased by Mr. Allan for three years for £90 per annum. At this time it had three public rooms and a shop with additional tables outside when weather permitted. Mr. Allan had been running a successful catering business at the beach before tendering for the lease of Hazlehead House. The house was demolished in the 1950s to make way for the present café.

759   FIRST TEES AND PAVILIONS HAZLEHEAD, ABERDEEN

A golf course was first proposed in 1923 when members of Aberdeen Town Council visited a site at Hazlehead. The course was constructed in stages with the first nine holes opened to the public in 1926. In 1927 a pavilion or clubhouse was proposed by the Links and Parks Committee at an estimated cost of £1,100. At the same time, a car park was discussed and later constructed. The clubhouse has been extended since that time but the original pavilion is still identifiable. In 1927 the cost of a round of golf was 1 shilling. The course was designed by Dr. Alister Mackenzie, famous worldwide for his courses and was fully opened in July 1927. In gratitude to Dr. Mackenzie, the championship course has been named after him. In 1930 a letter to the editor of the *Aberdeen Journal* complained of the lack of shelter if caught in the rain while out on the course. The letter was signed "Two Drookit Rats".

THE MAZE, HAZLEHEAD, ABERDEEN

58

Hazlehead Maze was planted in 1935 and is Scotland's oldest maze. Constructed of privet hedging, the maze was a gift to the people of Aberdeen by Sir Henry Alexander (1875-1940), Lord Provost of Aberdeen and was opened by Sir Henry's children, Gavin and Charlotte, in 1935. It measures 58m by 49m. Sir Henry was one of the Alexander family made famous locally by his father, also Henry, and his uncle, Dr William Alexander, both of whom were instrumental in the founding of the Aberdeen Press. Dr. William Alexander also wrote the famous North East Doric book – *Johnny Gibb of Gushetneuk*. Sir Henry died at his home, 31 Queen's Road now a nursing home in April 1940. The park employee standing on the platform, in the photo, directed people out of the maze if they got lost!

The No. 4 tram is seen leaving the reserved (private) trackway to Hazlehead. A separate parallel road to the north served other vehicles. Tram lines can be seen continuing on westward to terminate at Oldmill (later Woodend Hospital). The route from Sea Beach to Hazlehead was opened on 16th July 1924 as an extension to the tramway to Rubislaw. The line to Hazlehead was part-funded by the Scottish Office as a means of increasing employment opportunities for members of the armed forces who had been demobilized at the end of the First World War. Although the route had been served by buses since 1921 when Aberdeen Council acquired the Hazlehead estate, it was felt that trams with their additional seating capacity would be preferable.

Hazlehead tram terminus was one of two termini on this line – the other being at Woodend. Shown here are the double tracks merging into one at the tram shelter. The shelter is rustic in design with rough-hewn tree trunks as supports. The trams gave access to the Hazlehead public park, football and rugby pitches, the golf course and to the playing fields of Aberdeen High School for Girls (now co-educational Harlaw Academy) behind the shelter on the left of the photograph. The field to the right was used by the Royal Northern Agricultural Society's show in the 1950s.

One of the post-war Bogie Streamliners coming off the Hazlehead reservation. As smoking was allowed on the top deck, easy to clean leather seating was provided there while moquette upholstery was preferred for downstairs. The above car is a 1949 English Electric model numbered 34. The original Streamliners were expensive to run as they required two conductors – one to operate the doors and one to take the fares. Later some had their doors adapted to be opened and closed by the driver using compressed air. This route was discontinued in 1956.

Walker Dam off Springfield Road was part of an extensive early water management system to provide Aberdeen's water mills with constant water. It was one of a series of reservoirs damming the water of the How Burn or Holburn. Its outflow went eastwards through Johnston Gardens and continued on to provide power for the Upper and Lower Justice Mills. As the Justice Mills were mentioned in records of the Battle of Justice Mill in 1644, it is reasonable to suppose that the dam predates this time. It is thought that the name of the dam came from the Gaelic *uachdar*, or upper, dam. If true, this would infer that Gaelic was commonly spoken in Aberdeen at the time of the creation of the dam. It is generally accepted that this language was still spoken in Aberdeen in the 16th century, but died out soon after. The original church for the area was situated at Slopefield on Countesswells Road. It was made of iron and was known as the "Iron Kirkie". This church became too small after just 10 years so John Cardno Couper, the owner of the Craigiebuckler Estate donated land for a new stone church in 1882. The new church, seen above, was designed by Alexander Marshall MacKenzie and some of the bell metal from Auld Lowrie – the St. Nicholas bell cast in 1351 – was used to cast the bell for this church.

In the area now occupied by the hospital, there was a corn mill on the Denburn giving its name to the land known as Old Mill. This land was bequeathed to the city in 1839 by Dr. George Watt for the benefit of the poor. After some years, Oldmill Reformatory and Industrial School was founded in 1857 for the care and instruction of boys who had fallen foul of the law. The Reformatory was wound up in 1898. The buildings above were built as a poor house or workhouse for the whole of Aberdeen. It could house nearly 1,000 inmates in very basic conditions designed to discourage the poor from seeking shelter there. In the First World War, hospital accommodation was desperately needed to care for the masses of wounded men returning from the front. The 1st Scottish General Hospital was set up in Scotland. Oldmill was one of four hospitals under this umbrella organisation. However, Oldmill did not have sufficient accommodation for all the wounded, some of whom were in hastily-converted schools and some even in huts and tents. The photograph above shows a military pipe band providing entertainment. In 1927 the hospital was converted for civilian use and renamed Woodend. Unfortunately, older residents feared going to Woodend as they still remembered its days as a dreaded workhouse.

Oldmill Military Hospital, Aberdeen. Wounded and Nurses

Adelphi Series

A photograph of wounded soldiers and nurses at Oldmill or the Scottish General Hospital now Woodend. The nurses are from Queen Alexandra's Imperial Military Nursing Corps. This corps was formed in 1902 by royal warrant and has tended to sick and injured army personnel to this day. Their distinctive uniforms consisted of grey dresses with white aprons, white veils and red, or red and grey, capes. The red and grey capes were worn by reservists as seen in this photograph. At the beginning of the First World War there were just under 300 QA nurses but the heavy toll of casualties meant that by the end of the war, there were over 10,400 (including reservists).

Here we see wounded men in Hospital Blues, uniforms given to men recuperating in hospital. Their army uniforms were replaced by blue single breasted jackets and trousers with white shirt and red tie. They could also wear their service caps with regimental badges as can be seen above. The soldier standing on the right was David Angus Phimister, a private in the Army Service Corps. He drove an ambulance at the front until he was gassed in April 1918 and returned home to convalesce at the Scottish General Hospital now known as Woodend. He was my Grandfather.

This road, formerly known as Glenburn Road is now Rubislaw Den South and Spademill Road. In the first decade of the 19th century, a spade mill operated on the Denburn near this spot using the water power to operate hammers to form the metal blade. The property on the right was formerly a toll house and then a shop known as Rubislaw Supply Stores. The gate piers on the left flank the entrance to 40 Queen's Road giving access to it and No. 42 which were both built for Mr. F W Steele to a design by Matthews and Mackenzie. Rubislaw Toll House on the right was in operation between 1837 and 1865. In 1866 the toll house and garden were advertised to let. The toll house still marks the line of the old Skene turnpike. In the 1840s, Aberdeen had yet to expand west along the turnpike and fields of oats and potatoes were to be seen on either side of what is now Queen's Road.

This photograph was taken from Spademill Road looking north to the houses on Rubislaw Den South. At the back of these houses, there is a 14-acre communal park only accessible to owners of properties which back on to the Den through which the North Burn of Rubislaw flows. At the other end of Spademill Road at its junction with Queen's Road stands an old toll house now a restaurant. The house on the right is 6 Rubislaw Den South. It was designed by Robert Gordon Wilson in 1902 as were the two adjacent houses. They are all Category C(S) listed. It is said that 6 Rubislaw Den South is on the site of one of a cluster of houses called Hirpletillim. These simple dwellings have given way to grand homes. Near here stood the Glenburnie Distillery which produced whisky from around 1816 until 1875 when the buildings were converted into a photographic printing works by George W Wilson. This building has gone to make way for Forest Road. The Glenburnie Distillery used water from the Denburn in the distilling process and to provide power for grinding grain. A dam provided the means to control the flow. The distillery operated from the second decade of the 19th century until 1855 (when the lease was put up for sale) and produced 700 to 800 gallons of whisky per week. By 1864 it appears that no buyer had been found to take it over as a going concern and the buildings were put out to let for other purposes.

Rubislaw Den (south), Aberdeen.

A photograph taken from about 15/17 Forest Road on a dreich Aberdeen day. To the right is 2 Rubislaw Den South. Designed by Arthur Clyne and built by John Morgan in 1899, this imposing house stands at the junction of Rubislaw Den South and Forest Road. The houses to the left are a pair of semis Nos. 14 and 16 Forest Road. The side gable of No. 1 Rubislaw Den South is in the middle distance to the left of the photograph. This is a double villa, also designed by Arthur Clyne, and built around 1900. Further along on the right are Nos. 4 and 6 between which is a lane giving access to the Spademill Bridge over the North Burn of Rubislaw.

Rubislaw Den (North), Aberdeen.

Looking down towards Forest Road, this photograph of Rubislaw Den North seems to have been taken standing outside No. 20. Part of the estate of Rubislaw, this area was bought by the City of Aberdeen Land Association in 1877. In 1884, the Association sought permission from the council to extend Forest Road northwestwards to create a new street, later named Rubislaw Den North. All the houses seen here were built by John Henderson who lived at No. 10.

Rubislaw Den North, Aberdeen.   "Adelphi Series"

On the left of this view is 1 Rubislaw Den North with the photographer standing at the junction with Forest road. Number 1 was constructed in 1909 and is thought to be to a design by the architect, George Coutts, an Aberdeen architect. This exceptional house, constructed of contrasting pink and grey granite with a billiard room on the top storey is a Category B listed building. Adjacent is 3 Rubislaw Den North designed by A H L Mackinnon in 1896. This is a more austere house of grey granite. Originally a ten bedroom house, it has been divided into two substantial flats and is a Category C listed building. The horse drawn carriage is a hackney cab common at this time in Aberdeen.

The hospital in this photograph was originally called the Bellville Hospital for Incurables and was in Baker Street in the Denburn area of Aberdeen. However, in 1882, the town council purchased the property to construct Rosemount Viaduct. When the viaduct was complete, the area on both sides was feued (sold subject to an annual land tax and other restrictions) for as little as 10 shillings per linear foot frontage. The managers of the hospital bought a one and a half acre site in King's Gate – an elevated position in the suburbs of Aberdeen. The new Morningfield Hospital on King's Gate was designed by William Henderson and Son of Union Street, Aberdeen. It was built in 1883/84 of Rubislaw granite with lighter Kemnay granite band detail by George Ogg and Son and was originally called the Hospital for the Relief of Persons Labouring Under Incurable Diseases – more commonly, the Incurable Hospital. In its original form, Morningfield housed between 40 and 50 patients until a new wing was added in 1891 to provide additional beds. Unusually for the time, a lift was provided for 'the conveyance of feeble patients from one floor to another'. The hospital and grounds have since been redeveloped into flats.

A view of Rubislaw Quarry, often referred to as the deepest man-made hole in Europe. Derrick cranes for lifting the huge blocks of granite from the quarry floor can be seen at various points. A timber stairway is seen at the bottom of the photograph. These precarious ladders were the means of access to and from the quarry floor, a steep and arduous climb at the end of a long shift. Gibb supplied granite from Rubislaw Quarry for the construction of Sheerness Dockyard and lighthouses for Robert Stevenson, including the Girdle Ness and Cape Wrath lights.

This photograph shows men cutting granite with pneumatic drills. They are drilling holes along almost invisible grains in the stone. The holes were then enlarged to split the granite along the grain. This procedure was called plug and feather. The feathers were two shims inserted into the hole and the plug was then hammered between the feathers to create a crack in the granite. As was common at the time, men worked in boots, old trousers and jackets and flat caps with very little regard for personal safety. In the distance is what appears to be the Blondin Head. A Blondin was an aerial cable from which cradles carried men and granite around the quarry. The invention was named after Charles Blondin, a French tightrope walker and acrobat who crossed Niagara Falls in 1859 walking on a rope. John Fyfe of Kemnay is widely accepted as the inventor of the Blondin in the 1870s. Fyfe is said to have been inspired by watching a postman at Abergeldie pass mail across the River Dee on a loop of rope.

On the upper left of the photograph is a stone crusher fed by a system of cables lifting granite from the quarry face. In the centre is a cylindrical drum screen used to separate the crushed aggregates into various sizes. The aggregate fell down the four chutes to be collected at the bottom. It would appear that oversized material descended in the nearest chute while smaller aggregate – half to one and a half inch stone would come down the other three. The smallest aggregate, locally known as chuckies, would be used for paths. Carters are waiting to collect the granite at the bottom of the chutes.

Here is the interior of a typical granite workshed of the early 20th century. Until 1895, when pneumatic tools started to be used, all work on granite was carried out with hand tools. Although pneumatic tools increased output, it still took skilled men to operate the new equipment. In the workshed, stones were moved around either by crane or in bogeys on rails as seen above. The men on the left and right of the picture are holding bush hammers which were developed in the 1830s and are still in use in granite yards today. In 1911 individual tradesmen were paid only around 7d an hour and worked in excess of 50 hours a week. Because of the nature of the work, around 70% of the cost of dressed stone was labour. Up until 1895, worksheds were largely open to the elements with no protection for the workers. However, in 1895, Arthur Taylor carried out large scale improvement in his works in Jute Street including a completely covered shed and an 'Otto' Crossley gas engine with associated air compression chamber for pneumatic tools and gas lighting. The number of firms engaged in processing granite reached a peak of 96 in 1911.

This photograph shows men working with pneumatic tools to construct an elaborate Celtic cross. Hanging on the corrugated iron wall are two mason's squares for setting out accurate angles, and an array of chisels and squares sitting on the cross. Notice the lack of eye or ear protection! The tapered section at the base of the cross was made to insert into a slot in the plinth. Celtic crosses are commonly seen in Scotland and Ireland and are thought to have been faith symbols for many centuries. The Celtic cross design was used for many war memorials.

Desswood Place looking along to the junction with Forest Road. The construction of houses on this street began in the late 1880s and the road was widened to its present size in 1894 when 'desirable villas' were advertised for sale. Pavements were laid in 1898. In 1893 a newly-built property containing two tenanted flats was sold at the upset price of £850. The young postman in the picture is wearing knickerbockers typically worn by young teenagers in the early years of the 20th century. He is also wearing a dark blue shako cap with what appears to be a GPO badge on the front. The use of this type of copper alloy badge stopped in 1922.

HAMILTON PLACE, ABERDEEN.

Hamilton Place runs from Craigie Loanings to Forest Road and it was named after Dr. Hamilton, Professor of Mathematics at Marischal College. He took a great interest in everything concerning Aberdeen and was made a free burgess of the city. A number of the granite houses in this street have been listed as of architectural importance. All the listed buildings were designed by the architects Pirie and Clyne in the mid 1880s. J B Pirie designed his own house at No. 24 Hamilton Place. The photograph is probably dates from around 1905 going by the style of the pram.

An unusual view of side streets off Great Western Road. Ashvale Place is in the centre of the photograph looking eastwards towards Holburn Street. Great Western Place is on the right joining Great Western Road opposite Nellfield Cemetery. At the corner stands Beattie's licensed grocer listed in the directory for 1899. This shop had the agency for Stevenson Brothers Dry Cleaners, a coal merchant and Campbell's Cab Company. As usual for a corner shop, they sold anything and everything that the housewife might need. Further down Ashvale Place, the single storey shops included Kennerty's Dairy at No. 53. One of the girls is playing with a gird and cleek, a popular game in the early decades of the 20th century. It consisted of an iron hoop – the gird – with a looped handle – the cleek. Although it looks simple, it took skill to master the technique to keep the gird bowling along. There are several handcarts in the photograph. These were used by message boys and tradesmen to move bulky or heavy items around the town. Inserted into the side wall of the shop is a post box. It was obviously well used because a later model is still in place.

RSMITH ROAD

Great Western Road in the early years of the 20th century. In 1899 new streets were laid out in this area on land owned by the Aberdeen Hammermen Association, one of the Seven Incorporated Trades of Aberdeen. One of these new streets was Hammersmith Road on the left of the photograph. Building continued by various contractors well into the 20th century. Originally, Great Western Road was called Cuparstone Place at its junction with Holburn Street and Ashley Place to the city boundary. Then, at a meeting of land owners in the area in 1883, the names of Deeside Road, Cuparstone Road, Great Western Road and New City Road were all proposed and Deeside Road was decided by one vote. However, the town council went ahead with Great Western Road. The tram route to Mannofield opened in 1880 and closed in 1951. In the early years, trams would stop on demand but with electrification, Tramway Station signs on lampposts became the norm. Such a sign can be seen on the right at the entrance to Burns Road.

Shown here is the junction of Forbesfield Road, on the right, and Great Western Road. Forbesfield Road got its name from John Forbes, a Burgess of Aberdeen and a descendant of the House of Forbes of Newe in Strathdon. He acquired the land now known as Forbesfield around 1773. By the mid 1850s, Malcolmson Morrison was the tenant and used the land as a nursery to provide Aberdeen with fruit and vegetables. By the early 1890s feus for building houses were being sold. In the photograph, the shops at the corner of Great Western Road and Forbesfield Road are Thomas Robert Gordon, grocer at 364 Gt Western Road and William Smith, flesher or butcher at 366. They are both recorded in the 1908 directory. Gordon's grocer advertised Nectar Teas (in packets only) at 1s 8d to 2s 6d per pound in 1909.

Burns Road runs north from Great Western Road to Cromwell Road and was laid out in the 1890s. The name is usually thought to be a tribute to the poet, Rabbie Burns, but this was disputed by an anonymous councillor writing in the newspaper in 1891. He said that the committee could not think of a name until one of the members remembered that he had just received a letter from an address in Burns Road in another town. He suggested this name and it was agreed. Although the street was once lined with trees as was a feature of Aberdeen at this time, there are only a few of the originals left. However, in 1949, 40 new trees were planted at a cost of £2 per tree. This was part of a scheme to make Aberdeen a city of boulevards.

A tram on Great Western Road at Duthie Terrace with conductress and driver or motorman and just one passenger. This photograph was taken during the Great War. The poster inside the car behind the motorman reads 'The Kitchen is the Key to Victory'. Another advertisement is for the Clemak safety razor. At the back of the tramcar is a branch of the Northern Co-operative Society – telegraphic address 'Thrift'. The butcher and grocery departments were at the corner of Duthie Terrace Nos 497 and 499 Great Western Road. 'Take Me' matches, 3d a box in 1919, are advertised on the front of the tram. The tramcar is Aberdeen Corporation 81, built by Brush in 1914 as a Pay as you Enter Car with reversed stairs. It is also fitted here with folding windscreens meant to protect the motorman but when it rained, the top third could be flipped up – no windscreen wipers. It was rebuilt as a conventional car with vestibuled platforms 1923. On the far right of the photograph is a house that was still occupied in the 1960s and formerly known as Ruthrieston Cottage. Just beyond this house, but out of shot to the right, is the Mannofield Tram Depot and terminus for the Aberdeen trams.

This house was built in the 1880s probably for Stephen Paterson, a wholesale chemist in a family firm. He owned Amatola in the 1880s up to his death in 1896. The census of 1901 stated that the house had 15 rooms with windows. Paterson's wife, Frances Maria Paterson, was born in South Africa. Her father, John Paterson was born in Aberdeen and emigrated to South Africa in 1841 where he became a wealthy 'Cape Merchant', journalist and politician. His daughter named the house after the Amatola Mountains in South Africa. The house was put up to let in 1914 and remained as a family home until the 1930s when it was converted into an hotel. Latterly, it was the venue for a popular antiques fair. The house was said to be haunted by a lady in 19th century dress, allegedly resembling one of Stephen and Frances's daughters.

The southern end of Duthie Terrace was developed on land formerly owned by one of the Duthie shipbuilding family. It runs from Mannofield to Ruthrieston. Forty houses were given planning permission in 1894 but the street was not completely built up until between the wars. Further housing was built in the gardens of Cranford House in the latter part of the 20th century. The shop at 34 Duthie Terrace was a stationers and later a general grocer with a flat above accessed from Duthie Place. The shop property is now occupied by a development company. In 1896, a carpenter's shop, stables and a smithy stood near the top of Duthie Terrace on Great Western Road. The smithy had been occupied by James Mitchell until his death in the early 1850s. In the 1890s, the blacksmith was Robert Nicol. A house on this site was still inhabited in the 1960s. The tramway depot at the top of Duthie Terrace was built in the first decade of the 20th century. The site is now a flatted development. Note that even at this time when the houses are well established, the road is still compacted earth. The spire in the background is Mannofield Church.

Parish Church, Mannofield, Aberdeen.

Mannofield Congregation was first formed in the year 1881 in a temporary wooden building and the church building we know today was opened on 30th July 1882. The status as a parish church was granted in March 1882. Mannofield Church is situated in a prominent position on Great Western Road between Countesswells Road and Craigton Road. The building in grey granite, typical of the city, was designed by Jenkins and Marr, Architects, and was opened in 1882. Its steeple is the second tallest in Aberdeen. On the right of the photograph is the entrance to Duthie Terrace and, just out of shot is the tram depot. The tramlines can be seen crossing over towards the depot. Originally built as a horse tram depot, it became a depot for electric trams, then a plumber's merchants before being demolished to make way for flats. Trams were allowed to travel at 8mph on the straight but limited to 4mph on corners. With the advent of electric trams, the original single track with passing loops was doubled. In April 1902, when the line was electrified for the first time, several horses were startled!

This is the Cranford Road junction with Great Western Road. Cranford Road is on the left heading down to Ruthrieston. Great Western Road is going west into the middle distance with the provision shop marking the junction with Craigton Road. At the turn of the 19th-20th centuries, Cranford Road had only four new houses built on it next to Duthie Place. The shop on the left at the corner of Cranford Road, at 531 Gt Western Road, was operated by G and J.A M'Lean as a grocers shop and post office around 1910. The shop on the near corner was probably that of William Smith, grocer, who had the premises in the same year. Trams operated on this route on twin tracks from 1880 to 1951. They terminated just before this point at Mannofield Church. The suburban trams to Bieldside used the town twin track to Mannofield and thereafter used a single track with passing loops. The depot for suburban trams was at the corner of Morningside Road and Great Western Road.

This is Braeside or Braeside Farm in an area that was part of the Lands of Pitfodels held by the Menzies family for around 400 years. Braeside Farm stood on the North Deeside Road approximately opposite what is now Deeside Drive, west of the Mannofield Reservoir. The farm was mainly arable but was at one time a market garden. The house on the right looks to be the old farmhouse with an attached house or extension to the existing house of approximately Edwardian period. Sale particulars in 1953 mention only one house, steading and 55 acres. The Deeside Road was formerly known as the Deeside Turnpike and was described as a new road in 1802. As Aberdeen looked westwards to house the emerging middle classes, Braeside started to be feued and developed. Town gas was extended to the area in 1938. The majority of the housing in Braeside was built after the Second World War. In the late 1940s, a new five room detached granite house on Springfield Road, Braeside could be bought for only £1,050. How times and prices have changed.

This photograph shows the interior of the old crematorium at Kaimhill. Built in 1937 and designed by Robert Leslie Rollo, it is a Category B listed building. It was closed in 1975 when the new Aberdeen Crematorium was opened at Hazlehead. Aberdeen City Council first discussed the building of a crematorium in 1899 but it did not become a reality until 1938. The council still did not agree to fund the building and it was left to private investors to found a new company – Aberdeen Crematorium Ltd. On the opening day in March 1938, 3,400 people were given the guided tour of the facility. This private company operated the crematorium at Kaimhill until 1944 when the council bought out the shareholders. The building with its handsome timber-lined ceiling and panelling to dado height, is now owned by a funeral director.

Looking from Holburn Street west along the street called Union Grove. Plans for a new street, later to be called Union Grove, were passed in 1886 along with plans for Ashvale Place running parallel to and south of Union Grove. However, the western part of Union Grove was named Grove Street on an 1888 map. The house called Union Grove was the home of Gavin Hadden, a wealthy manufacturer. He was born in Aberdeen in 1770, the son of Baillie Alexander Hadden and his wife Elspeth Young and died at Union Grove in 1857. Gavin Hadden was provost of Aberdeen for four terms of office. A large part of the estate was put up for sale in 1858 at an upset price of £7,000 although the house remained the home of the Hadden family for some time thereafter. Later, it became a school for girls when Miss Isabella Duncan and her sister moved from their previous premises at 13 Union Row. Later, they moved again to Albyn Place to found St. Margaret's School for Girls. The shop at the far right of the photograph is that of Mr. W Matthews, grocer, who ceased trading in 1912 so this photograph must predate that. After 1912 the shop became a dairy. The shop next to that is W T Michie's tobacconist and stationer, 6 Union Grove, which was trading in 1910. Between the two shops is an enamel sign advertising an Agent for Thomson's Dye Works, Perth. The church to the left of the photograph is St. Nicholas, Union Grove, built in 1887/88 to a design by G Wilson of Ellis and Wilson. It is a Category C listed building that has now been converted into flats.

Originally, a road called Grove Street ran from Forest Road in the west to the site of this junction where it took a near right angled turn northwards to meet Albyn Place opposite the junction of Queen's and Rubislaw Terraces. That part of Grove Street that ran northwards was renamed Albyn Grove in 1889 with the remainder running from Holburn Street to Forest Road named Union Grove. The above photograph shows the junction with Union Grove with Albyn Grove. In 1926, while the shop at the corner was operated by Mr. Thomas Oliver Cowell, the large plate glass window was smashed by a frightened horse pulling a potato merchant's cart. The horse ended up inside the shop causing a great deal of damage. The animal was cut by the glass but not too seriously. The driver and the merchant were unhurt. Mr. Cowell had been a Sergeant Instructor with the Aberdeen Volunteer Artillery and would appear to have been a veteran of the Afghan War of 1878-1880. The second shop on the left was the Grove Dairy. The curious building in the middle distance with the arched first floor window is now part of a garage.

This is Union Grove at Albyn Grove. Far left, next to the tenement door, is Charles Chree's chemist shop and then a fruiterer on the corner with Albyn Grove. The fruit shop boasts a public telephone at a time when home landlines were rare. Chree's shop is still a chemist at the time of writing. It is interesting to note that this Charles Chree was a cousin of another Charles Chree, the eminent physicist who was superintendent of the Kew Observatory from 1893 to 1925. The houses and shops on the right of the photograph have been demolished and replaced with new flats in a sympathetic style. Prior to the construction of these streets, this area was a marsh through which the How Burn ran on its way to power the Justice Mills. The shop beyond the junction on the left is 124 Union Grove where William Anderson was a grocer and wine merchant.

A scene of Union Grove looking east from about the junction with Annfield Terrace. On the right is the entrance to Brighton Place. The shop at the near corner of Brighton Place used to be a grocer's in 1910. The shop on the other corner, 291 Union Grove was a chemist's in 1910. Three well-dressed boys are standing in the street with a man behind. The cart on the right is drawn by a Clydesdale horse with a distinctive white blaze. This breed of horse was favoured for their calm temperament and strength.

In this view, the photographer is standing in Union Grove looking west. To the left is Ashley Road and to the right is St. Swithin Street. The house on the left is now a shop with a door in the bay window. The shop on the far right has the name Alexr Smith above the door. In the 1911 directory, Alexander Smith had a stationer's shop at this address with James Farquharson, grocer at the corner and J Lindsay, chemist just out of shot. The boy standing in St. Swithin Street is in charge of a handcart. He is unusually well dressed for a message boy so may have been posed for the photograph.

Ashley Road, named after Ashley House, is seen here at its junction with St. Swithin Street and Union Grove. The road has been straightened since this photograph was taken. Along with Mannofield, Robert Balmanno purchased this land in 1772. As a Quaker (or Friend), he named his home Friendville and the small farm on his land he named Friendship Farm. The name is perpetuated in Friendship Terrace, a small group of former farm workers' houses just off Ashley Road. Friendship Farmhouse can still be seen on Ashley Road. The land for Ashley Road Public School was feued to the city by John Cook, shipowner, of Ashley House in 1886 on condition that drainage work was carried out on the site. This was probably required to alleviate flooding from the West Burn of Rubislaw which took water from Rubislaw Quarry and the surrounding area. Ashley Road School can be seen to the right of the photograph in the middle distance. This school was of a similar design to Rosemount School but with improved ventilation.

A view of Forest Avenue which runs between Great Western Road and Cromwell Road. This was taken taken at around No. 59 on the left. In 1919, a flat in this street could be rented for £17 per annum. As there appears to be a gap site at the far right, it would seem that the photograph was taken before the present chalet bungalows were built. In 1923 the Ordnance Survey map indicates a large area of open ground at the end of the terrace of tenement properties on the right. At that time, Annfield Terrace was a cul de sac off Union Grove. By 1938 Annfield Terrace had looped round to join Forest Avenue south of this point.

This is Devonshire Road looking east. In the far background, the tenements of St. Swithin Street can be seen. The street was built in the late 1890s. The photographer appears to be standing at the entrance to Union Grove Lane. The street comprises terraced properties, many of which are purpose built flats, and some semi-detached houses. When first constructed, the average price was £700. Devonshire Road was one of several politically inspired street names. They included Beaconsfield Place (Benjamin Disraeli's title was Earl of Beaconsfield), Hartington Road (the Duke of Devonshire was also Marquess of Hartington) and Gladstone Place.